fabric art projects

Susan Stein

fabric art projects

**Fashion and Décor Items Made from
Artfully Altered Fabric**

Susan Stein

**Creative Publishing
international**

www.creativepub.com

dedication

To my dad, C. Emmett Shogren, who was my greatest supporter and encouraged me to accomplish whatever I set my mind to.

To my husband, John, for forty-one years of love, support, and encouragement.

Creative Publishing international

First published in the United States of America by
Creative Publishing international, Inc., a member of
Quayside Publishing Group
400 First Avenue North
Suite 300
Minneapolis, MN 55401
1-800-328-3895
www.creativepub.com

ISBN-13: 978-1-58923-444-4
ISBN-10: 1-58923-444-8

Printed in China
10 9 8 7 6 5 4 3 2 1

Library of Congress Cataloging-in-Publication Data

Stein, Susan, 1945-
  Fabric art projects : fashion and home décor items made from artfully altered fabric / Susan Stein.
      p. cm.
  Includes index.
  ISBN-13: 978-1-58923-444-4
  ISBN-10: 1-58923-444-8
  1. Textile crafts. 2. House furnishings. 3. Interior decoration. I. Title.

TT699.S693 2009
746--dc22

2008050785

President/CEO: Ken Fund
Vice President/Sales & Marketing: Kevin Hamric
Publisher: Winnie Prentiss

Copy Editor: Karen Levy
Proofreader: Alissa Cyphers
Book Design: Tina R. Johnson
Cover Design: Tina R. Johnson
Page Layout: Tina R. Johnson

Acquisition Editors: Linda Neubauer, Deborah Cannarella
Production Managers: Laura Hokkanen, Linda Halls
Creative Director: Michele Lanci-Altomare
Senior Design Managers: Jon Simpson, Brad Springer
Design Manager: James Kegley
Photographer: Joel Schnell
Photo Coordinator: Joanne Wawra

contents

introduction

Embellishment, surface design, and **painting** on fabric are fun techniques that encourage you to release your **creativity.**

It is enjoyable to play with the art supplies and do small samples, but now you can make practical and lovely items for your home or for personal use and you don't have to wait for large blocks of time. This book will give you many choices of items to make for yourself or for gifts. All that is required is a playful "what if" attitude and the equipment you probably already have in your home.

Decorative items for the table include candle covers made from gorgeous silk fiber, jar covers that turn canning jars into colorful vases, a lovely painted tea cozy, and monoprinted placemats that can be coordinated with any décor. For personal use, you can make a binder cover with an inkjet transfer, a fabric bead necklace, a paintstiked apron, a rusted silk scarf, a fun lunch bag, or a unique brayer-painted folder briefcase. For your home, make a silk throw for pure luxury, an artful discharged dye pillow, screen-printed pillowcases, a fun mail sorter with family photos, a collaged wall hanging, or a screen that shows off different painting techniques. When you're elbow-deep in all this creativity, tell your friends what you've been doing with exciting fabric postcards. Many of the techniques are interchangeable, so feel free to swap techniques to suit your projects.

As you play with these techniques, remember that there is no right or wrong way to do things. It is far better that items show the mark of the maker than for things to look "factory perfect." Get together with your friends to share ideas, tools, and supplies, and have a ball.

Susan L. Stein

gossamer silk candle cover

Use a variation of the gossamer silk technique to decorate your home with a colorful and unique accessory.

Sewing the fibers to a piece of heat-resistant template plastic and adding other embellishments gives you a translucent cover for a candle. The light can be seen through the needle holes and the thin spots in the fiber. Make one version with lace and ribbon, another with a painted motif under the fibers, and a third with beaded trim along the top edge.

materials and tools

- plastic cover for the table
- measuring tape or ruler
- roving: silk, viscose, nylon, or other non-felting fibers in roving (combed, not loose) form
- templar heat-resistant template plastic
- embellishments: lace, ribbons, silk pieces, or artificial leaves and flowers
- scissors
- water-soluble stabilizer: Sulky Super Solvy
- sewing machine
- large sewing machine needle: Jeans #16
- cotton decorative thread

- darning foot (optional)
- sink or other container for water
- lace or beaded trim
- zipper foot
- strong glue: Fabri-Tac
- two or three large rubber bands
- two clothespins or clamps
- votive candles in aluminum holders
- rubber stamp
- paint: Jacquard Neopaque
- sponge brush: 1" (2.5 cm)
- iron

gossamer silk candle cover

Preparation
Cover your work surface with plastic.

Pull lengths of fiber from the silk skein about 11" (28 cm) long by holding your hands that far apart and pulling gently. Separate the fibers into thin wisps and lay them parallel over the surface of a piece of template plastic, keeping the layer thin so light will show through.

Lay lace, ribbons, silk leaves or flowers, or other trims onto the surface of the fibers. You can add a few more wisps of fiber if you like. Make sure all embellishments are colorfast in water, because you will be rinsing the candle cover to remove the stabilizer.

3

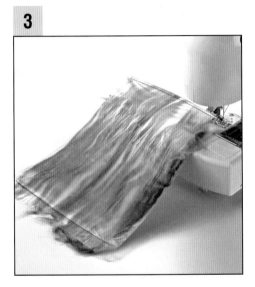

With scissors, cut a piece of Super Solvy slightly larger than the template plastic and lay it over the fibers, pressing out the air between the layers. Using the large sewing machine needle and decorative thread, sew along the shorter edges of the plastic to secure the Solvy and fiber ends.

Note: The fibers and embellishments will shift slightly as you work. Use a longer stitch length to prevent the plastic from tearing between stitches. Use sturdy cotton thread to add interest and withstand the heat of the candle.

4

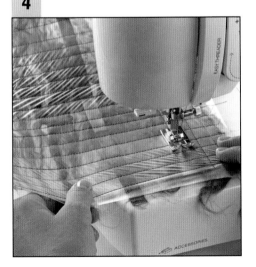

Use a straight stitch to make a ½" (1.3 cm) grid of stitching or meander-stitch with a darning foot all over the surface of the fiber sandwich, catching all trims and fibers in the stitching. Trim the excess fiber and stabilizer from the edges.

Continued

5

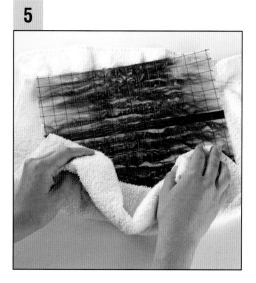

Soak the fiber sandwich in warm water for 10 minutes, then drain the water and run water over the piece to remove all traces of the stabilizer, which will feel slippery if present. Blot with towels and allow to dry.

6

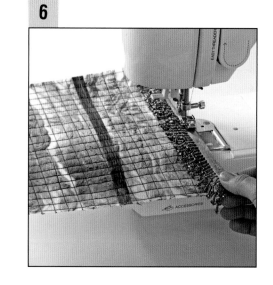

If you are using a beaded trim on the top edge, sew it on after the fibers are dry. Use a zipper foot so you can sew close to the beaded edge. Allow for a ½" (1.3 cm) overlap on one edge.

7

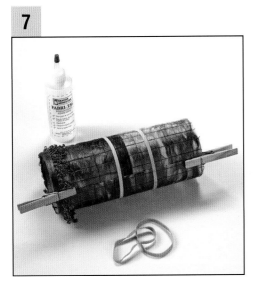

Overlap the edges of the template plastic ½" (1.3 cm) and glue in place. Place rubber bands around the middle and clamps at the ends of the candle cover while it dries to keep the overlap even and in contact with the underside edge. Remove the clamps and bands and place the finished cover over a votive candle.

8

For another look, rubber stamp a motif onto the template plastic using Jacquard Neopaque paint. With a sponge brush, dab paint onto the rubber stamp and stamp onto the plastic sheet. Let the paint dry thoroughly, iron the plastic from the back with a medium-hot iron to set the paint, and then layer the fibers over the painted motif as described in steps 1 to 5. Finish as in step 7.

Note: Hand-dyed silk and viscose roving by Diane Bartels.

Susan Suggests

Place the votive candle in its holder on a heatproof coaster to protect your table and light your candle cover all the way to the top.

inkjet transparency to book cover

Use a copyright-free image, a favorite photograph, or one of your own drawings to decorate a removable album cover.

Use any inkjet copier or computer printer to make a transparency, and then burnish the ink onto fabric that's been painted with gel medium. The resulting image will be slightly distressed and is a nice alternative to the perfect look of a photo transfer done directly onto fabric. This method should be used on projects that will not be washed.

materials and tools

images: copyright-free images, photographs, drawings, or text

inkjet copier or computer printer

inkjet transparency sheets (available at office supply stores)

plastic cover for the table

tape

small piece of fabric for background of transfer

paint brush

gel medium: Golden regular gel, matte finish (available at art supply stores)

bone folder (optional)

iron and press cloth

three-ring binder or book to cover

measuring tape or ruler

scissors

cover fabrics: ½ yd. (0.5 m) each for outside and inside of book cover

sewing machine

thread

pins

embellishments (optional)

fusible quilt batting (optional)

inkjet transparency to book cover

Preparation
Cover your work surface with plastic.

1

Look for an image that will fit nicely on the size book you wish to cover. Dover books are excellent sources for copyright-free images and can be found at any bookstore. To start, choose a small to medium-size design so you can practice transferring all the lines to the fabric before the gel medium dries out. You can place several small images on one transparency and cut them apart if you like. Make the inkjet copy or printout on the rough side of the inkjet transparency sheet.

2

Tape the background fabric to the plastic-covered work surface. With a brush, spread gel medium onto your background fabric quickly and evenly, brushing in both directions. Make sure the area covered is larger than your image. The fabric should be wet but not overly so, or the transparency will slip and the image will smear. Run your finger over the fabric to check for places that are not covered.

3

Place the transparency facedown on top of the wet gel medium and burnish the image onto the fabric with a bone folder or your fingernail. Use circular motions and be sure to cover every area, working quickly while the medium is still wet. Check to see the results by carefully lifting a corner. You won't get a perfect transfer, but that is the beauty of this method. Remove the transparency sheet, which should have very little ink left on it, and let the medium dry completely. Turn the dry transfer right side down on a press cloth and iron from the back to flatten it.

4

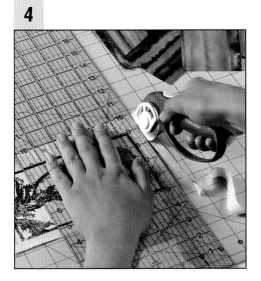

Measure the binder or other book when it is opened up and laid flat. Add 1" (2.5 cm) to the width and length for ease and seams. Decide how big to make your transfer piece and trim it to that size, adding ¼" (6 mm) seam allowances on all sides. Cut pieces of the outside cover fabric to border the transfer so it will be centered on the front of the cover and go around the back cover, adding extra to the size of the border pieces for seams and optional quilting.

Tip: Make a rough sketch of the pieces to cut so you can check your measurements.

Continued

5

Sew the outside cover pieces to the four sides of the transfer piece with ¼" (6 mm) seams, pressing the seam allowances away from the transfer. Add any embellishments at this point. You may wish to add batting and quilt the outer cover. Trim it to the size determined in step 4.

6

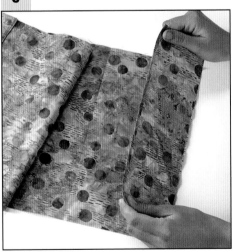

Cut a lining piece the same size as the outside cover and two lining pieces the height of the cover by 4" (10 cm) wide. Sew under ¼" (6 mm) on one long side of the two lining pieces. Lay the two strips right side up on the right side of the lining, with the hemmed edges toward the center.

7

Lay the outer cover right side down over the lining and strips. Pin. Sew a ¼" (6 mm) seam around the edges, leaving a 3" (7.5 cm) opening in the stitching on the bottom edge of the back section. Press under the seam allowances of the opening and clip the corners.

8

Turn the cover right side out through the opening and stitch or fuse the opening closed. Press the book cover, lay it flat, and insert the binder or sketchbook into the flaps.

Susan Suggests

Embellishments you might consider: fabric foil, piping around the transfer piece, beading, collage, rubber-stamping, or Paintstiks. Fusible batting makes it easy to quilt the outside cover without adding another piece of fabric on the back.

lasagna painted silk throw

There is nothing that feels as lovely as silk, but did you know it can be less expensive than cotton?!

Look for China silk, silk twill, crinkle chiffon, silk with motifs woven into it, organza, and other silks that have similar weights. Pile up squares of the different pieces and pour on Dye-na-Flow paint. Walk away for a few hours, and then peel apart the layers to reveal gorgeous colors and patterns. Back the squares with batting and a print fabric, quilt along the printed motifs, and you have the makings of the most luxurious throw you've ever seen!

materials and tools

plastic cover for the table

silk fabrics: twelve 22" (56 cm) squares of various natural-colored silks, all of similar weights (8 to 12 mummie)

plastic pipettes or eyedroppers

paints: Dye-na-Flow by Jacquard (I used golden yellow, azure blue, and brilliant red)

iron

clothes dryer

batting: Hobbs queen-size fusible

rotary cutter, acrylic ruler, and mat

cotton fabrics: six ⅝ yd. (0.6 m) pieces of coordinated cotton fabrics for backing (should have large patterns that can be quilted around)

sewing machine

darning foot

thread

quilting gloves (optional)

scissors

ribbon: 10 yd. (9.15 m) to match painted silk, 1" (2.5 cm) wide and straight-of-grain

binding fabric: ½ yd. (0.5 m)

lasagna painted silk throw

Preparation

Cover your work surface with plastic. If you are unfamiliar with this technique, experiment on a small stack of silk fabrics before you begin your project.

1

Collect silks of several different weaves and patterns, keeping in mind that you want it to have a little body (about the weight of a typical silk scarf) so it will be easy to handle. Cut or tear twelve 22" (56 cm) squares of fabric. You will be cutting down the size slightly after the quilting is completed. Press all creases out of the silk because the paint will follow them. Divide the silk pieces into three stacks of four pieces each. Do not pin them.

2

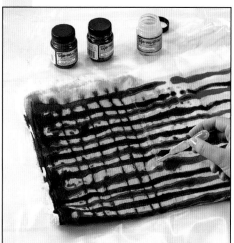

Using a separate pipette or eyedropper for each color, dribble paint onto the top piece of each stack. Create a grid or other pattern that covers much of the fabric but leaves some white space, since the paint will flow for some time after you apply it. The bottom layers will collect a lot of paint, so too much paint will make the colors muddy, but not enough paint will leave too much white on the top layer. Work quickly so the colors blend. For variety, use a different order or pattern on each stack. Note that different silks have different absorbency rates, regardless of their thickness.

3

After the paint is completely dry, carefully pull the layers apart. Heat set the paint by ironing each piece for 3 minutes, or throw the pieces in the clothes dryer on high for 30 minutes.

4

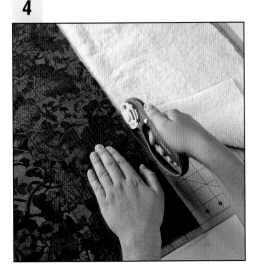

Place the fusible batting in the dryer for 5 minutes on delicate to remove the wrinkles and preshrink it. Preshrink the backing fabrics by ironing them with steam. Use a rotary cutter, ruler, and mat to cut the backing fabrics into twelve 22" (56 cm) squares and fuse them to the batting using lots of steam. The other side of the batting will stick to your ironing surface, but it peels off readily. Trim the batting to fit.

Continued

lasagna painted silk throw (continued)

5

Steam-iron the silk pieces to the other side of the batting sandwiches. Sizes may not match exactly, but the squares will be trimmed after the quilting is completed.

6

Drop the feed dogs on your machine and put on the darning foot. Quilt around the motifs on the backing fabrics (you don't have to follow the lines on the print exactly). Remember that the bobbin thread will be what shows on the silk side of your quilt sandwiches. Make sure the density of the quilting remains fairly consistent from one sandwich to the other. Wearing quilting gloves helps you move the sandwiches more easily.

7

After quilting, cut the sandwiches down to 20½" (52 cm) square. Arrange the pieces in four rows of three sandwiches, balancing the colors and patterns. Sew the pieces of each row together with ¼" (6 mm) seams, stitching through all the layers. Sew the seams with the backing sides together so the seam allowances show on the silk side. Press the seam allowances open, as flat as possible. Sew the rows together, matching seam intersections.

8

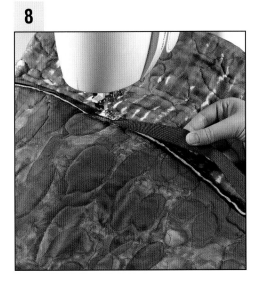

Center the ribbon over the seams on the silk side, covering the seam allowances. Sew close to both edges. The back of the quilt will have sewn lines parallel to the seams. After all the seam allowances are covered, bind the quilt.

A quick and easy variation: Buy a pre-hemmed silk scarf blank, 12" x 60" (30.5 x 152 cm), and fold it into five 12" (30.5 cm) sections. Paint the top layer, let it stand until dry, unfold, and heat set. A designer scarf for under $5!

Susan Suggests

If you can't find ribbon to match your painted silks, buy white ribbon and paint it with the same colors as your fabrics. Remember that paint, unlike dye, can be used on any fiber content, so you can use polyester or rayon ribbon if you like. Remember to heat set it just like the fabric, using a temperature appropriate for the fiber.

fabric bead necklace

Can't afford diamonds? Make a necklace every bit as exciting out of fabric you probably have in your stash.

Now you can have matching accessories for every outfit in your closet. There are all sorts of ways to embellish your beads and no end to the colors and styles you can make. Remember that you can also use fabric beads for garment closures, purse latches, tassels on scarves, three-dimensional elements on collages, and any number of other uses.

materials and tools

rotary cutter, acrylic ruler, and mat

fabrics: ½ yd. (0.5 m) tight weave and saturated color (batiks work well)

iron

fusible web: $1\frac{1}{8}$ yd. (1 m) Wonder-Under

bamboo skewer

leather or rattail cord: $2\frac{1}{3}$ yd. (2.1 m)

foil adhesive

cotton swab

foil for fabric

decorative yarns or trims

embellishments: wire and glass beads

silk dupioni

fabric glue

mixed media: felt or wooden beads, charms, or ribbons

fabric bead necklace

1

Using a rotary cutter, ruler, and mat, measure and cut the fabrics into four 10" x 17" (25 x 43 cm) pieces. Fuse Wonder-Under fusible web to the back of each piece, using a dry iron.

2

Cut 33 strips 1½" (3.8 cm) wide and 10" (25 cm) long. Cut the strips into long triangles, centering the point at one end and angling to the corners of the opposite end. Remove the fusible web release paper from the back of the strips.

3

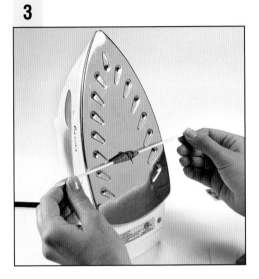

Lay a strip, fusible side up, on the work surface. Starting at the wide end, roll the strip on a bamboo skewer, ending with the narrow point. Hold the bead against a hot iron and roll it to melt the fusible web, making sure you catch the point securely. Heat the bead until it is firm, but do not melt the bead to the skewer. When cool, slide the bead off the skewer.

4

Repeat step 3 for all the fabric strips. Cut three lengths of cord to 24" (61 cm), 28" (71 cm), and 32" (81 cm). String nine beads on the short cord, eleven beads on the middle cord, and thirteen beads on the long cord. Tie all of the ends together in a square knot; the strands will fall in a cascade.

Continued

fabric bead necklace **29**

Foil

If you want to add a little glitz, leave the bead on the skewer and apply dabs of foil adhesive to the surface of the bead with a cotton swab. Stick the point of the skewer into something and allow the adhesive to dry. Then, place a piece of fabric foil over the dry adhesive, color side up, and use the iron to burnish the foil onto the bead. Turn the bead and reposition the foil until all of the adhesive is covered. Glitter and glitter glue also work well.

Embellish

Add interest and texture to your beads by winding them with yarns and trims. You may want to add a tiny bead of glue to the knot if the trim is slippery. Or wrap a piece of wire around the bead and add small glass beads to the wire ends.

Silk

Use dupioni silk to make lustrous, fringy beads for a dressy outfit. Do not back the fabric with fusible web because you want the edges to ravel. Simply cut the silk into long triangles, roll onto the skewer, and secure the points with fabric glue.

Mixed Media

Combine your fabric beads with felt or wooden beads, charms, or ribbons. Make the strips longer or wider for larger beads.

Susan Suggests

You could also string your beads onto yarn, fishing line, fine silver chain, or ball chain. If you choose to use $1/8$" (3 mm) satin cord for stringing, make your beads using a chopstick or dowel rather than a skewer so the hole in the bead will accommodate the larger diameter cord.

Colorful Quilts
2233 Energy Park Dr.
St. Paul MN 55108

Art washes away
from the soul
the dust of
everyday life.

painted fusible web postcards

Everyone enjoys getting mail that is colorful, creative, and fun.

These simple fabric postcards can be mailed with a first-class stamp. For a little extra postage, you can add an amazing amount of embellishment.

Make personal fabric postcards for all occasions and keep some on hand for quick greetings and gifts.

materials and tools

- rotary cutter, acrylic ruler, and mat
- fusible web: Mistyfuse
- plastic sealable bag
- measuring spoon
- powdered pigments: Pearl Ex by Jacquard
- fabric: black and white print or plain black
- cooking parchment (available at grocery stores)
- iron
- foil for fabric
- very stiff interfacing: Timtex or Peltex

- paper-backed fusible web: Wonder-Under
- embellishments: printed fabrics, ribbons, silk leaves, lace, trims, buttons, and beads
- hand-sewing needle
- netting (optional)
- backing fabric: sturdy white cotton
- rubber stamps (quotations work well)
- ink pad
- fabric pen
- sewing machine
- thread: variegated and white

painted fusible web postcards

With a rotary cutter, ruler, and mat, measure and cut a piece of Mistyfuse 7" (18 cm) wide. Place it in a large plastic sealable bag and add about ½ teaspoon of Pearl Ex powder. You may use more than one color, but they will blend rather than give two distinct colors when applied to the web. Close the bag and shake to distribute the pigment powder fairly evenly onto the web.

Cut a piece of fabric the same size as the painted Mistyfuse. Place the web over the fabric and cover with cooking parchment. Use a dry iron to press the web onto the fabric. Make sure the web is securely attached to the fabric so that the foil in the next step does not pull it off.

3

Place a piece of fabric foil, color side up, over the painted web. With the edge of a dry iron, rub over the foil sheet quickly three or four times to transfer the foil to the web. Light strokes will give you a better look than heavy ones. Leave some areas without foil for contrast.

4

Cut a piece of stiff interfacing and a piece of paper-backed fusible web the size of the fabric. Using a dry iron, press the paper-backed fusible onto the interfacing, let cool, and pull off the backing paper. Iron the painted fabric onto the fusible web, using a piece of cooking parchment over the fabric to protect the iron. Cut the fabric/interfacing piece into four 4½" x 6½" (11.5 x16.5 cm) rectangles. You will trim them to their final size later.

Continued

5

Cut out motifs from printed fabrics or choose ribbons, silk leaves, skeleton leaves, lace, and trims that coordinate with the painted web, foil, and background fabric. Place the items on the postcards, cover with cooking parchment, and fuse in place. If the Pearl Ex and foil have exhausted the adhesive properties of the Mistyfuse, place another piece of web under the motifs, ribbons and so on.

6

Trim the cards to an exact 4" x 6" (10 x 15 cm) rectangle (U.S. postal requirement). Do seed stitching by hand or add machine-stitched details. Sew embellishments such as buttons or beads to the postcards by hand or machine. Make sure that any decorations are very firmly attached to the cards. Even if you ask for hand cancellation at the post office, the cards will still go through various machines on the way to the recipient. One way to protect delicate embellishments is to cover the whole front of the card with netting.

7

Make four backs for the cards from sturdy white cotton cut 4½" x 6½" (11.5 x 16.5 cm). On the left side of the fabric, rubber stamp a quotation using ink or use a fabric pen to write a personal message and add your return address. On the right side of the backing piece, put the recipient's address. For postcard exchanges, I use photo transfer fabric sheets to print the return address multiple times and make a sheet of recipient's addresses, which can then be applied to the back of the card with fusible web when the postcard is completed.

8

Center a postcard front over a backing piece with wrong sides together. Set the machine for satin stitching and thread the machine with variegated thread on the top and white or variegated thread in the bobbin. Satin stitch the edge of the postcard and then trim off the excess backing fabric. Use a self-adhesive stamp on the back and burnish it onto the fabric securely with your fingernail. Drop your postcards into a mailbox and prepare for rave reviews!

Susan Suggests

Gather a group of friends and have a postcard exchange. Set a deadline and decide on a theme—otherwise, anything goes! One of the best exchanges I've been part of was based on dots. Imaginations ran wild with everything from yellow polka-dot bikinis to quilt pox to elegant dots made from satin.

discharged dye pillow

A fun technique to try is discharging dye, which removes color rather than adding it.

It can be done with a variety of products using many different applications of the chemicals. Be sure to work in a well-ventilated area or outside. It is common to work with black fabric, but other colors also work well. Batiks, with their multiple layers of dye, produce wonderful results. For this project, you will apply a paste that can be used on all fibers, unlike bleach, and can be used with fewer precautions than chlorine. The color is removed with an iron through an almost magical process.

materials and tools

plastic cover for the table

rotary cutter, acrylic ruler, and mat

fabric: ½ yd. (0.5 m) of cotton batik

iron

stencil with large open areas (some of the discharge paste will seep under the stencil, so choose one without fine details)

sponge brush: 1" (2.5 cm)

discharge paste by Jacquard

batting: 13" (33 cm) square

backing fabric: 13" (33 cm) square

sewing machine

thread

pillow fabric: ½ yd. (0.5 m) of heavier weight coordinating homespun, corduroy, or silk matka

pins

16" (40.5 cm) square pillow form

discharged dye pillow

Preparation
Cover your work surface with plastic.

1

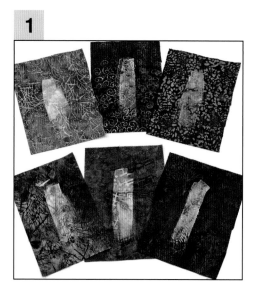

Test several different fabrics to determine which discharges the best, what colors emerge, and what matches your décor. Lay out swatches of each fabric, brush on discharge paste, and let dry. You won't see any change in color as it dries. Iron the fabric and watch as the color mysteriously disappears. You may rinse the fabric if you wish, but it is not necessary.

2

With a rotary cutter, ruler, and mat, measure and cut a 12½" (32 cm) square piece of the batik fabric to be discharged. You may want to discharge two squares so you can choose the best one. Make sure the fabric is pressed smooth. Cut the main pillow fabric into two 2½" x 12½" (6.5 x 32 cm) strips, two 2½" x 16½" (6.5 x 42 cm) strips, and two 12" x 16½" (30.5 x 42 cm) back panels.

3

Make sure the room is well ventilated. Place the stencil in the center of the batik piece and brush discharge paste through the openings. Wash the paste out of the brush and off the stencil and let the fabric dry.

4

After the paste is completely dry, place the batik piece on an ironing board and iron it until all the areas have changed color, moving the iron around so you don't get impressions of the steam holes.

Continued

5

Place the batting and backing piece behind the batik fabric and, with a sewing machine, quilt around the stenciled motif to add dimension and strengthen the batik. This will also make the weight of the panel more comparable to the weight of the main pillow fabric.

6

Sew the two 2½" x 12½" (6.5 x 32 cm) strips of the main pillow fabric to the top and bottom edges of the batik panel with a ¼" (6 mm) seam allowance. Press the seams away from the center. Sew the two 2½" x 16½" (6.5 x 42 cm) strips of pillow fabric to the sides of the batik panel. Press the seams away from the center.

7

Turn under one long edge of a back panel piece ¼" (6 mm) and press. Turn under again 1" (2.5 cm), press, and stitch. Hem one long edge of the other panel in the same way. Place the pillow top right side up on the table and place the two backing pieces, right sides down and overlapped, onto the pillow top, so the raw edges match. Mark the corners of the backing pieces so they are rounded. Pin the edges and sew a ½" (1.3 cm) seam all the way around. Trim the corners. Turn the pillow right side out and insert the pillow form.

More Ideas

Apply the discharge paste to a foam stamp and stamp it onto the fabric. Or simply brush the discharge paste onto the fabric using a foam brush. Use masking tape to make a resist of straight lines. Use the discharged fabric for simple potholders or a pocket for a tote.

Susan Suggests

If you want more precise edges in your stenciling, spray stencil adhesive on the back of the stencil and let it dry. The tackiness of the adhesive will help hold the stencil in place on the fabric. Alternatively, make your stencil from freezer paper and iron it onto the fabric temporarily.

paintstik decorated apron

Use oil paint sticks and a rubbing plate to decorate a butcher apron with a colorful design.

Shiva Artist's Paintstiks come in many colors and are easy to use. Once they dry and are properly heat set, the color is permanent. Choose matte or iridescent colors, apply them easily, and iron to set the color.

materials and tools

plastic cover for the table

apron fabric: 7/8 yd. (0.8 m) pant-weight cotton

iron

scissors

nonslip sheet: Grip-n-Grip

rubbing plates

paintstiks: assorted colors

paper towels or small knife

cooking parchment (available at grocery stores)

bias tape: one package (3 yd. [2.75 m]) wide double-fold

pins

thread: to match apron and bias tape

sewing machine

heavy cardboard

craft knife

glue for cardboard

paint for cardboard: house paint, textile paint, or acrylic

paintstik decorated apron

Preparation

Cover your work surface with plastic. Protect your carpet and clothing, because any flakes of paint that fall from the work surface will dry and become a permanent stain.

1

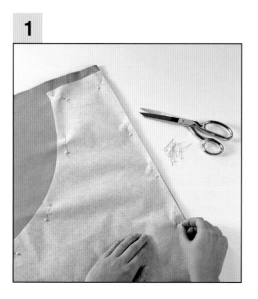

Rinse the apron fabric to preshrink it and remove sizing and wrinkles. Press. Enlarge the pattern on page 49 and use it to cut out the apron.

2

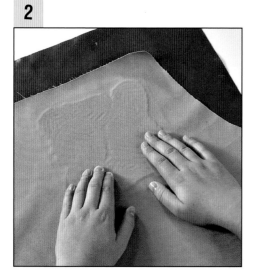

Place the nonslip sheet on the table. Choose one or more rubbing plates and arrange them on the sheet. Cover the plates with the apron faceup. Use your hands to press the apron onto the rubbing plate so you can tell where the edges of the design are located.

3

Peel off the protective skin that forms on the flat end of the paintstik, either by pinching it off with a paper towel or trimming it off with a small knife. Carefully dispose of the peelings so they don't get on your clothes or floor. Place your left hand firmly down on the left side of the area of the apron to be decorated to hold it in place. Rub over the area covering the rubbing plates with the paintstik, trying not to go beyond the edges of the raised designs and stroking in one direction, away from your left hand. (Or switch hands and directions if you are left-handed.) Let the apron dry undisturbed for two to three days, depending on how heavily the paintstik was applied.

4

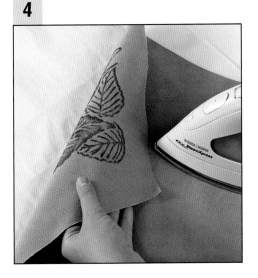

Protect your ironing surface with cooking parchment. Place the apron facedown and iron with a dry iron for 10 to15 seconds in each spot that was decorated. Make sure the room is well ventilated. This will make the paint permanent to washing, but the apron (or any project colored with paintstiks) should not be dry-cleaned.

Continued

paintstik decorated apron **47**

5

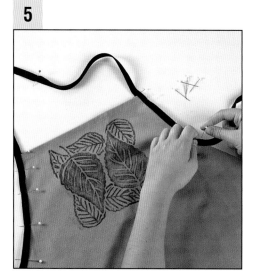

Turn under the top edge, long sides, and bottom edge of the apron ¼" (6 mm); press. Turn under ½" (1.3 cm) again; press and stitch. Fold the bias tape in half to determine the center. Place the tape around your neck so the center mark is in back and mark the tape where you want the top edge of your apron. Pin the bias tape around the remaining raw edges of the apron, with the wider fold on the back of the apron. Align the marks with the top edge, creating a neck strap, and extend the ends beyond the sides to make ties. Sewing from the right side, stitch the tape along the full length.

Custom Rubbing Plates

To make your own rubbing plates, start with a large square of cardboard and then cut a design out of a second piece of cardboard, using a craft knife. Glue the design to the square, weight it down with books, and let dry. Or glue string or kids' letters to the cardboard. Paint the entire surface of the cardboard to seal it and let dry. Use as a rubbing plate as described in step 3. Other household items, such as trivets, can also be used as rubbing plates.

Susan Suggests

Paintstiks are the perfect medium to grab for embellishing a project that needs a little spark, such as a wall hanging with a plain border or an ordinary sweatshirt cut up the front to make it a unique jacket.

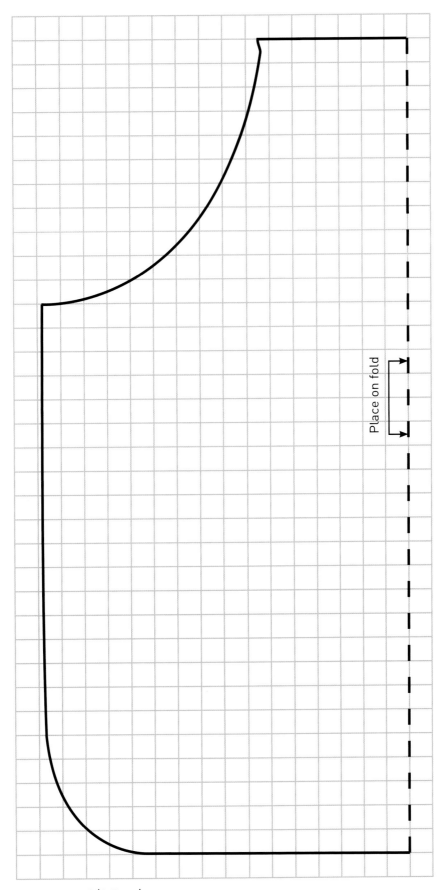

Place on fold

1 square = 1" (2.5 cm)

angelina jar wrap

Angelina "hot fix" fibers are synthetic fibers that will fuse to each other when heat is applied.

They are very shiny, come in luscious colors, and can trap other fibers and embellishments when they are formed into a sheet. For a fun project, make a jar wrap and display flowers or other items in it or make a cone to hang. Be sure to protect your iron from touching the fiber and prepare to have a sparkly sewing room and clothing!

materials and tools

small canning jar or mayonnaise jar

tape measure

pencil

string

cooking parchment
(available at grocery stores)

fiber: Angelina "hot fix" in several colors
or one sampler pack

iron

scissors

embellishments: sequins, trims, fibers,
bits of silk

ribbon: several ⅛" (3 mm)-wide ribbons,
approximately ½ yd. (0.5 m) of each plus
some for snippets

stiff piece of paper: 8½" x 11"
(21.5 x 28 cm)

tape

clear-drying glue

angelina jar wrap

1

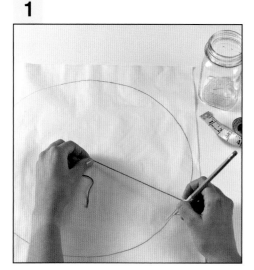

Measure your jar by running a tape measure down the side, across the bottom, and up the opposite side. Allow for 2" (5 cm) extra to make the ruffle around the top. I used a 14" (35.5 cm) circle. Draw a circle with your final measurement as the diameter onto a piece of cooking parchment, using a string taped onto a pencil as a compass. It does not have to be a perfect circle, because it will be used only as a pressing guide.

2

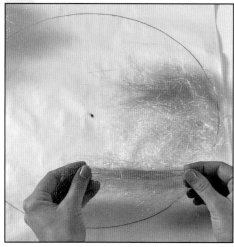

Pull apart the Angelina fiber and lay it out on the parchment paper in a thin layer, using as many colors as you wish. Make sure you cover the circle over the drawn lines and cross the fibers over each other. Too thick a layer will require too much heat to melt the fibers and the colors will change and dull.

3

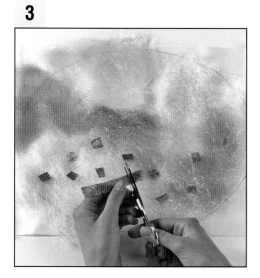

Make a small sheet of Angelina fiber in a contrasting color by using an iron to fuse it quickly between sheets of parchment paper. Cut it into small squares or other shapes. Distribute the sequins, trims, or cut-up bits of Angelina over the unmelted fiber.

4

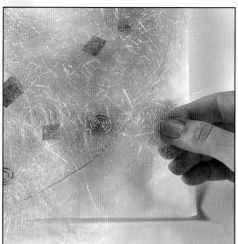

Add a small amount of Angelina fiber on top of the embellishments so they will be firmly caught in the Angelina sheet when it is melted.

Continued

angelina jar wrap (continued)

5

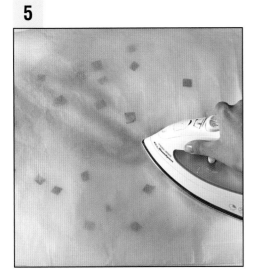

Cover the Angelina with another sheet of cooking parchment and heat the surface with an iron set for silk or wool (irons vary, so experiment with the temperature). The Angelina should fuse to itself and capture the other embellishments.

Note: The more time and pressure you put on the iron, the more the color of the Angelina will change. It is possible to turn the Angelina completely black, but it is more likely that you will just dull the color if you leave the heat on too long. Do some testing before you make your jar cover.

6

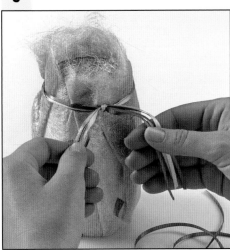

Place the jar in the center of the circle of fused Angelina, pull the sheet up around the jar, and tie the ribbon around the top of the jar. Use several narrow ribbons together for a different look, or use some of the exciting knitting ribbons and add charms to the ends.

1

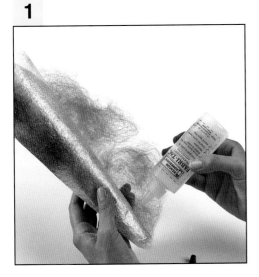

Angelina Cone

Make a pretty cone of Angelina to hang on a tree, decorate a window, or serve as a delightful party favor. Following the steps above, make a circle of Angelina fiber 12" (30.5 cm) in diameter or smaller. Make a cone of stiff paper and tape it together for a form. Wrap the fused circle of Angelina around the form and glue it along the edge.

2

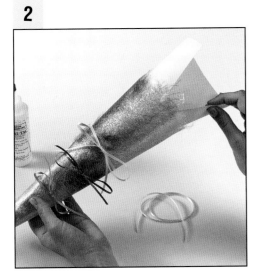

Wind the cone with ribbons and glue them in place. Make a hanger out of ribbon and glue it to the top of the cone. Add trims as desired, and then remove the paper form.

Susan Suggests

After it is fused into a sheet, Angelina fiber can be foiled, painted, burned along the edges, and further embellished. Spend a little time exploring!

screen-printed pillowcase

What child wouldn't love to have a personal pillowcase? Make one from fun fabric and screen print the child's name on the hem band.

Or make some artful pillowcases for your own bed, possibly matched to the quilt or a painting in the room. Although some techniques for making the screens are more high-tech, this method of screen printing is easy to do and the materials are readily available.

materials and tools

plastic cover for the table

pillowcase fabric: ⅞ yd. (0.8 m) cotton

accent fabric: ⅓ yd. (0.32 m)

iron

rotary cutter, acrylic ruler, and mat

printing screen, approximately 10" x 12" (25.5 x 30.5 cm) (available at art supply stores)

duct tape

cleanser and toothbrush

sticky-back plastic shelf liner: 10" x 12" (25.5 x 30.5 cm)

commercial letter stencils (optional)

craft knife

newspaper

paint: Neopaque by Jacquard

credit card or screen-printing squeegee

old towel

small paintbrush

sewing machine

thread

screen-printed pillowcase

Preparation

Cover your work surface with plastic.

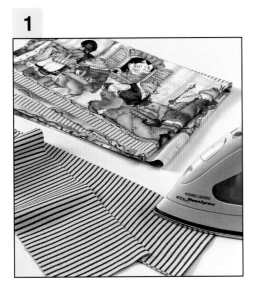

1

Preshrink the fabrics and iron them smooth. Using a rotary cutter, ruler, and mat, measure and cut the main fabric to 27" x 40" (68.5 x 101.5 cm). Cut the hem band 9" x 40" (23 x 101.5 cm). Press the hem band in half in both directions, wrong sides together, to mark the position for printing.

2

Cover all the wood of the printing screen frame with duct tape, extending the tape onto the exposed mesh about ½" (1.3 cm); repeat the taping on the other side of the frame. Scrub the mesh with cleanser and a toothbrush to open all the holes in the weave completely. Rinse and dry thoroughly.

3

Draw your design or stencil your lettering on the protective paper side of the shelf liner. Make sure your design will fit into a 3½" x 8" (9 x 20.5 cm) space. Use the craft knife to cut out the design. If you want to include a name plus another motif in a different color, cut two stencils and use two screens.

4

Pull off the protective paper from the shelf liner and press the sticky side to the back of the screen (the side that will lie flat on the fabric). Your lettering should read correctly when the screen is laid on the fabric.

Continued

5

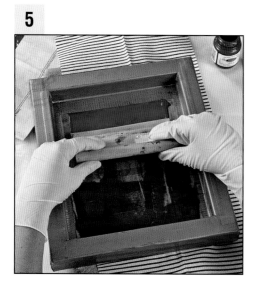

Place a pad of newspaper on your plastic-covered table. Turn the screen so the stencil is flat against the paper. Pour one or two colors of paint onto one end of the screen and squeegee it across the screen so the design in the stencil is printed clearly onto the paper. It might take a little practice to determine how much pressure is needed: too little will not put enough paint on the paper and too much will push paint under the openings in the stencil.

Place the hem band on an old towel, making sure the design is centered on the correct quarter section of the hem band, and screen print the design onto the fabric.

6

Carefully pull the screen straight up and off of the fabric. Touch up any missed spots with a small paintbrush. If you are only making the one print, remove the shelf liner from the screen immediately and wash the screen with a brush to remove all traces of paint. Let the painted fabric dry thoroughly. If you are using two screens, add the additional motifs, let dry again, and then iron the fabric for 30 seconds with a hot iron to set the paint.

7

Sew the hem band to the main fabric, with the right side of the hem band against the wrong side of the main fabric. Sew with a ½" (1.3 cm) seam allowance. Press the seam toward the hem band. Press under ½" (1.3 cm) on the other edge of the hem band, fold it over to the front to make a band, and topstitch it over the previous seam.

8

Fold the pillowcase in half, right sides together. Sew the long side seam and the end opposite the band with a ½" (1.3 cm) seam. Trim the seam. Zigzag or serge the seam allowances together to prevent raveling. Turn the pillow case right side out and press.

Fabric: Tidings and Tales by J. Wecker-Frisch
Licensed to Wilmington Prints

Susan Suggests

Tuck a piece of lace or folded strip of fabric into the seam when you topstitch the band of the pillowcase for a special accent.

burned-edge appliqué tea cozy

Make a pretty accessory for your table or sideboard with painted silk and burned-edge appliqué.

Dye-na-Flow paint makes it easy to add vibrant color without the complexity of dyeing, and it keeps the soft hand of the fabric. Since you are painting "blobs" on a large piece of fabric and then tearing it into strips, all of the colors blend. The blackened edges lend a nice contrast to the brightness of the silk. This technique could also be used for a lovely vest.

materials and tools

plastic cover for the table

fabric: ¾ yd. (0.7 m) of natural color 12 mm silk twill or other silk with body

spray bottle filled with water

paint: Dye-na-Flow by Jacquard

sponge brushes:1" (2.5 cm)

silk salt or other coarse salt

iron

scissors

batting: cotton/polyester

sewing machine

thread: to match cozy and invisible for appliqué

walking foot

pins

candle in tip-proof holder

large tweezers or forceps to hold silk in flame

container of water to douse burning silk if it gets out of control

darning foot

lining fabric: ⅜ yd. (0.35 m), cotton

burned-edge appliqué tea cozy

Preparation
Cover your work surface with plastic.

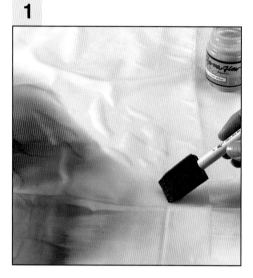

Tear the silk into one ½-yd. (0.5 m) and one ¼-yd. (0.25 m) piece. Lay the larger piece on the plastic-covered work surface and spray it with water. Brush on Dye-na-Flow paint with a sponge brush straight from the jar, or dilute the paint for a lighter look. Paint irregular areas of color rather than a pattern. To make the colors blend, make sure the silk is quite wet—spray it again after painting if you wish. Use colors that mix well, such as blue and yellow, red and blue, or red and yellow, or the three printer's primaries (magenta, turquoise, and yellow), as in the sample.

Sprinkle silk salt over the surface of the painted silk and allow it to dry undisturbed. Walk away and do something else because the process takes about 45 minutes to work. When you return, you will be amazed at how the salt has attracted the paint, making streaks and circles. Allow it to dry completely. Brush off the salt.

3

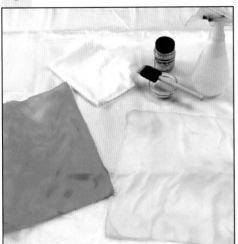

Tear the smaller silk piece into four 9" x 11" (23 x 28 cm) pieces. Lay out the pieces on the plastic and spray them with water. Paint two of them in shades of green for leaves; paint the other two in flower colors that contrast with your background piece. Allow them to dry. Iron all of the silk pieces for 30 seconds on each area to set the paint. Wash and dry the large piece to remove the salt residue and iron smooth.

4

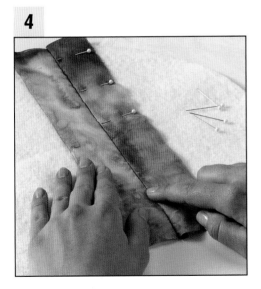

Draw a done-shaped pattern 14" (35.5 cm) wide and 11" (28 cm) tall. Use it to cut two pieces of batting. Tear the large piece of silk into strips about 2" (5 cm) wide. Place two silk strips right sides together in the middle of one batting piece and sew along one edge through all the layers with a ¼" (6 mm) seam allowance, using the cozy thread and a walking foot. Finger press the top strip over onto the batting and pin.

Continued

5

Continue to sew new strips, right sides together with the previously sewn strips, until half the batting is covered. Then cover the other half in the same manner. Sew the strips at an angle if you wish so the widths are irregular. Repeat for the other piece of batting. Trim the fabric even with the batting. Sew around each piece ⅛" (3 mm) from the edges to stabilize them and prevent them from raveling.

6

Cut the small pieces of silk into very rough flower petal and leaf shapes. Place a candle firmly in a holder and set it next to a container of water. With the tweezers or forceps, hold each petal and leaf in the side of the candle flame to singe and seal the edges. Avoid the top of the flame because it will put soot on the silk. Gently blow out any flames that are burning too far into the pieces.

Note: Douse the silk in the water if the flame gets out of control.

When cool, pull off any hard charred bits of silk.

7

Arrange the silk petals and leaves on the tea cozy halves and pin them in place. Topstitch close to the edges, using a darning foot and invisible thread. Place the two completed halves right sides together and sew the curved edges together with a ¼" (6 mm) seam. Turn right side out.

8

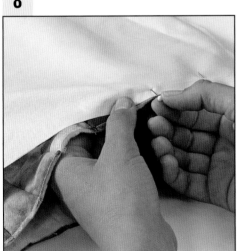

Cut two lining pieces according to the pattern and sew right sides together along the curved edges, leaving a 3" (7.5 cm) opening in the middle of the curve. Slip the lining over the silk piece, right sides together, and sew all around the straight bottom edge. Turn the tea cozy right side out through the opening in the lining, and sew the opening closed. Tuck the lining up into the inside of the tea cozy. Topstitch the bottom edge, if desired.

Susan Suggests

Remember that any folds or wrinkles in the plastic under the silk will also make patterns in the paint. When you tear the silk into strips, you can eliminate any portions that you wish.

monoprinted placemats

Monoprinting is a very old method for printing on paper, using ink and a marble slab.

Today we can print our own fabric using textile paint and a piece of plastic or glass. First you apply paint to the surface and manipulate it. You can use many methods for drawing in the paint—all fun and rather playful. Then you lay the fabric over the paint and roll over it to transfer the design. Often you can get a second print from the paint that is left over, and sometimes it's better than the first! When the paint is dry, heat set it with an iron, and make some great new placemats for your table.

materials and tools

plastic cover for the table

center fabric: ½ yd. (0.5 m)

border/backing fabric: 1⅓ yd. (1.2 m)

batting: cotton/polyester, crib size

iron

rotary cutter, acrylic ruler, and mat

masking tape

piece of template plastic or glass with taped edges: at least 10" x 14" (25.5 x 35.5 cm)

permanent black marker

paint: Lumiere by Jacquard

sponge brushes: 1" (2.5 cm)

rubber or foam stamp

paper towels

soft rubber brayer (available at craft and art supply stores)

spray bottle filled with water

one 12" x 16" (30.5 x 40.5 cm) piece of mat board or heavy cardboard

pins

sewing machine

thread

monoprinted placemats

Preparation
Cover your work surface with plastic.

1

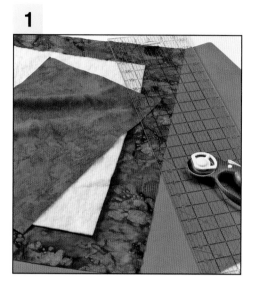

Preshrink the fabrics and batting. Iron the fabric smooth. With a rotary cutter, ruler, and mat, measure and cut four 9" x 13" (23 x 33 cm) pieces of the center fabric. Cut four 17" x 21" (43 x 53 cm) pieces of the border/backing fabric. Cut four 12" x 16" (30.5 x 40.5 cm) pieces of batting.

2

Tape the plastic or glass to the table to make it easier to pull the fabric off the paint. Draw a 9" x 13" (23 x 33 cm) rectangle on the plastic with a marker. Apply the Lumiere paint to the plastic within the drawn rectangle with a sponge brush. Try to apply enough paint to minimize brush marks but not so much that the paint will spread out everywhere when you print the fabric. But, as always, imperfections show the mark of the artist and are what make your work unique! Work quickly so the paint does not dry on the plastic.

3

With the stamp, pick up paint from the plastic by pressing down hard and lifting straight up. Wipe the stamp on paper towel between each use. Randomly stamp until there is pattern all over the painted area. Work quickly so the paint does not dry.

4

Lay the center fabric facedown on top of the paint, being careful not to smear the design. Roll the brayer over the top of the fabric so the paint transfers to the fabric. Pull the fabric straight up off the plastic and set aside to dry. Repeat the process for three more pieces of fabric. Heat set the paint by ironing the fabric on the back with a dry iron for 30 seconds on each area.

Continued

Print Variation

To make two prints from one paint setup, spray water onto the paint that remains on the plastic after printing the first piece of fabric. Lay a second piece of fabric over it. Roll the brayer over the fabric to transfer the paint. The second print will be much lighter and show the pattern of the spray.

5

Press under the edges of the border/backing fabric ½" (1.3 cm) all the way around. Center the mat board on the wrong side of the border/backing, and press the edges up and over the board. To miter the corners, first fold in the corner diagonally and press. Then fold in the sides to meet in the center of the corner. After pressing, remove the mat board.

6

Place the batting piece in the center of the border/backing aligning it to the outer the folds. Center the printed piece over the batting, tucking the edges under the folded edges of the border. Pin.

7

Topstitch the edges of the border through all the layers. Quilt the center around the printed motifs if you wish.

Susan Suggests

Use the monoprinting technique to make a table runner. Follow the same steps, adjusting the measurements to suit your project. Make napkins with satin-stitched or serged edges to match.

rust-dyed silk scarf

Beauty can come from humble beginnings. Although rust stains are something we usually avoid, this project promotes them!

The wonderfully rich-colored surface of this silk scarf was created by staining it with rust. After being trapped inside a plastic bag with wet metal findings and steel wool fibers, a once plain scarf emerged as a truly unique work of art. Soon you will be searching nooks and crannies and even the street for castoff metal pieces with interesting shapes.

materials and tools

plastic cover for the table

nongalvanized metal objects: washers, gears, architectural elements

plastic or metal tray

rubber gloves

nongalvanized steel wool

hemmed silk scarf: 9" x 54" (23 x 137 cm) or size of your choice

spray bottle

vinegar

garbage bag

heavy books

basin

measuring cup

salt

wire cutters

stovepipe wire

sandpaper

PVC pipe, about 12" (30.5 cm) long

rust-dyed silk scarf

Preparation

Cover your work surface with plastic.

1

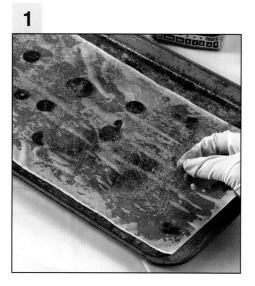

Place some of the metal objects in the tray. Put on the rubber gloves to protect your hands and shred some steel wool over the bottom. Fold the scarf to fit into the tray over the metal objects. Spray the scarf with a solution of half vinegar, half water. It should be quite wet.

2

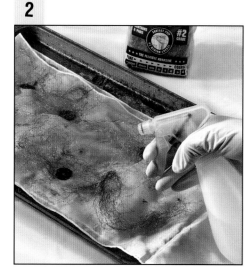

Lay more metal objects on the top layer of the scarf. Shred more of the steel wool, sprinkling it over the entire surface. Spray the metal with the vinegar-water solution.

3

Place the tray in a garbage bag and close the end. Weight the metal objects down with heavy books so they maintain good contact with the scarf. Place the tray in a warm place for 24 hours or until you like the amount of rusting (sometimes as little as 2 hours makes a nice design).

4

Wearing the gloves, remove the tray from the plastic bag and take off all of the metal objects and steel wool. In a basin, mix ¼ cup (60 ml) of salt in 4 gallons (16 l) of hot water. Soak the scarf to neutralize the rust. Wash the scarf in soapy water, rinse, and dry.

Continued

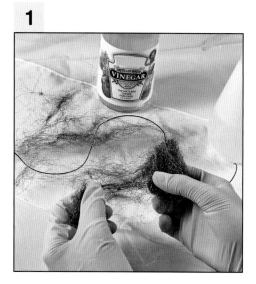

Rust and Wrinkles

For another look, lay the scarf out flat on a plastic-covered table. Spray it with vinegar-water. Cover the surface with shredded steel wool.

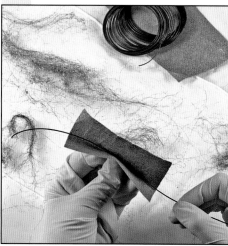

Cut a piece of stovepipe wire several inches longer than the length of the scarf. Fold a piece of sandpaper in half and run the wire through it to remove the protective coating. Lay the wire down the length of the scarf.

3

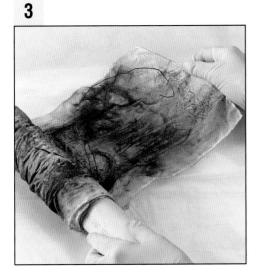

Roll the scarf onto a PVC pipe, curving the wire as you go. Wrap any remaining wire around the scarf to hold it on the pipe. Scrunch the scarf together sideways to create wrinkles. Spray with vinegar-water again. Place in a garbage bag for 24 hours or until the rusting is complete. Unwrap the scarf from the pipe, neutralize, wash, and dry.

Rusted Cotton Scarf

Scrunch hand-dyed cotton fabrics and layer them in a plastic zipper bag with steel wool and vinegar-water. Allow the fabric to rust. Wash and dry the fabric. Cut it into 3½" (7.5 cm) squares. Sew them together in 24 rows of three squares, and topstitch the outer edge. Wash or brush the seam allowances to fray them, for a casual look.

Susan Suggests

If you use rust-dyed fabric for piecing or appliqué, be aware that the fabric will be harder to stitch through. Use a microtex/sharp needle.

brayer-painted lunch bag

If your idea of packing a lunch is to throw a beverage and a frozen entrée into your briefcase, here's a great idea for you!

This attractive, insulated lunch bag is also a conversation-starter at work or on the bus! Brayer painting over textured items makes a unique fabric for the outside layer. A dense quilt batting provides the insulation, and a tightly woven cotton lining resists snags from silverware. Make lunch bags for the kids too, using their plastic letters and other toys for rubbing patterns. Better yet, have them make their own bags!

materials and tools

plastic cover for the table

rotary cutter, acrylic ruler, and mat

outer fabric: ½ yd. (0.5 m)

batting: 12" x 32" (30.5 x 81 cm), fusible cotton/polyester by Hobbs

½ yd. (0.5 m) of cotton fabric (such as batik)

textured items: rubbing plates, bamboo placemats, plastic lace, kids' letters, leaves, etc.

tape: double-stick and masking

paint: Neopaque or Lumiere by Jacquard

large plastic plate or a piece of template plastic or glass for rolling out paint

soft rubber brayer (available at craft and art supply stores)

iron

sewing machine with zigzag stitch

thread

Velcro: 3" (7.5 cm)

brayer-painted lunch bag

Preparation
Cover your work surface with plastic.

1

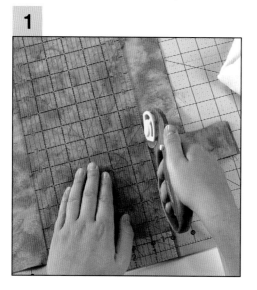

With a rotary cutter, ruler, and mat, measure and cut 12" x 32" (30.5 x 81 cm) pieces of outer fabric, batting, and lining fabric.

2

Lay out textured items on the plastic-covered table so they cover a 12" x 32" (30.5 x 81 cm) area. Use double-stick tape to hold them in place.

3

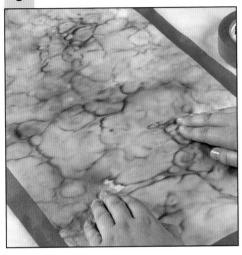

Place the outer fabric over the textured items and tape the edges to the plastic-covered table, using masking tape. Rub your fingers over the fabric so you can make a slight imprint where the rubbing materials are located.

4

Pour paint onto the glass or plastic palette, and roll the brayer through it until there is paint evenly distributed around the roller in a thin layer.

Continued

5

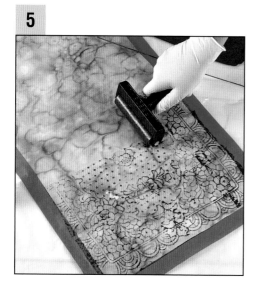

Working quickly so the paint doesn't dry, roll over the fabric in the shorter direction, reloading the brayer for every pass. Let the paint dry. Iron the fabric on the back with a dry iron to set the paint.

6

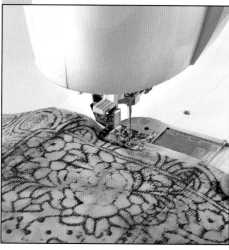

Layer the outer fabric, batting, and lining. Fuse the layers together by steaming, first from one side and then from the other side. Follow the batting manufacturer's directions. Set your machine for a fairly wide satin stitch and sew all around the edges of the quilt sandwich.

7

Fold the quilt sandwich in half, right sides together, aligning the short ends. The short ends will become the top of the bag. Stitch the sides with a ¼" (6 mm) seam. To make gussets at the bottom, flatten the bottom, forming triangles on each side, with the side seams centered in the triangles. Sew across each triangle, perpendicular to the seam, 2" (5 cm) from the point.

8

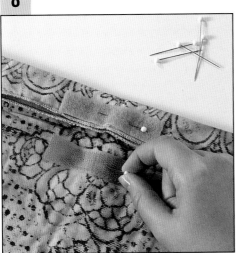

Turn the bag right side out. Center a piece of Velcro loop tape along the top edge of one side; stitch it in place. From the opposite side, fold down both sides of the upper edge twice, 1½" (3.8 cm). Mark where the hook tape should be. Unfold the bag and stitch the hook tape to the outside of the bag.

Susan Suggests

Practice loading and using the brayer before starting your project. It is difficult to get an entirely even application of the paint because the brayer puts down more paint on the first revolution of the roller, but putting too much paint on will blur the rubbing completely.

collaged wall hanging

Quilts are becoming more and more personal, not just in color selection and labeling, but also in composition.

Collage allows us to collect all sorts of elements and embellishments that convey a message or mood and then sew them onto a small background piece using relaxed methods of construction. Celebrate an event, portray an emotion, remember a vacation, or just enjoy using your favorite images. Then display your collage on the wall where it will be enjoyed daily. Start collecting!

materials and tools

prints: screen prints, sun prints, rubber-stamped images on fabric

fabric: odd blocks, hankies, special cuts of print fabric, accent fabrics

embellishments: buttons, skeleton leaves, feathers, shells, ribbons, yarns to couch, lace, trims such as "eyelash"

beads, including fabric beads (see page 27)

photo transfers on fabric

background fabric: fat quarter (approximately 18" x 22" [45.5 x 56 cm])

iron

rotary cutter, acrylic ruler, and mat

border/binding fabric: ⅝ yd. (0.6 m)

fusible batting

backing fabric: ¾ yd. (0.7 m)

black fabric

scissors

pins

threads: decorative, invisible, beading if using glass beads

sewing machine

hand-sewing needle

clear-drying fabric glue

permanent marking pen

inkjet copy machine

collaged wall hanging

Collect orphan quilt blocks, small sun prints and screen prints, rubber-stamped images, ribbons, lace, buttons, beads, photos transferred to fabric, skeleton leaves, yarns, etc. that coordinate in theme, color, or mood. Put them up on the design wall with possible choices for background fabric.

Press and straighten the background fabric. For the border, cut three 3" (7.6 cm)-wide strips using a rotary cutter, ruler, and mat. Cut 25" x 29" (63.6 x 73.5 cm) pieces of batting and backing fabric. Cut 2" (5 cm)-wide strips of binding fabric.

3

Lay the backing fabric on the batting, and fuse together with steam. Turn over and steam-fuse the background fabric in the center of the batting. The borders will be added later. Place the quilt sandwich on the design wall.

4

Arrange the larger elements such as the screen prints, sun prints, old quilt blocks, etc. on the background. To make these items pop out visually, center them over black fabric cut ½" (1.3 cm) larger. Remember the art theory that odd numbers look better than even numbers. Vary the sizes and shapes of your elements. Use diagonal lines and on-point placement for interest. Keep in mind that you will be adding more embellishments, so don't fill every space. Pin the elements in place.

Continued

5

Connect the larger elements with ribbons, yarn, or other directional items. You want to unify all the various parts of the collage, carrying the viewer's eye around the piece and holding her interest. Some of the ribbons or yarns can go under the larger units and some can go over the sides or edges. Pin everything in place.

6

Choose threads that coordinate or contrast with the parts of the collage. Stitch ⅛" (3 mm) in from the edges of the larger units, appliquéing and quilting in one operation. Stitch down both sides or down the middle of the ribbons. Stitching down the middle will raise the edges and give more dimension. Stitch over the yarns with a zigzag stitch and invisible thread.

7

Cut one strip of border fabric in half, and trim it to the exact horizontal size of your background piece. Place the top and bottom border strips right sides together with the background fabric and sew through all the layers with a ¼" (6 mm) seam. Open up the border strips and steam to the batting. Sew the side borders on in the same way.

8

Add smaller embellishments such as cut squares or triangles, leaves, or appliqués, extending them onto the borders, if desired. Sew around the edges of each unit or use detail stitching to attach them, such as using veins in a leaf to sew it down instead of edge stitching. Trim and bind the edges of the wall hanging and add a casing to the back for hanging. Hand-sew or glue fragile or hard elements such as skeleton leaves, beads, buttons, and feathers. Sign and date the wall hanging with a permanent pen.

Susan Suggests

Fresh flowers or three-dimensional items such as rocks or shells can't be stitched to your collage, but you can still include them. Lay them directly on an inkjet copy machine, print a fabric sheet, and add the print to your collage instead.

painted tabletop screen

A small accordion-folded screen, displayed on a table or bookshelf, is a pretty way to show off your favorite painting techniques.

This screen was designed using different types of Jacquard paints. The techniques include resist painting, painting a plaid, sun printing, salt patterning, bubble wrap printing, and painting over pleated foil. Add quotations or poetry with Mistyfuse web and ExtravOrganza inkjet fabric sheets, if you like.

materials and tools

plastic cover for the table

fabric: 9" x 11" (23 x 28 cm), white and colored

masking tape

paint: Lumiere and Dye-na-Flow by Jacquard

sponge brushes: 1" (2.5 cm)

masking objects: leaves, paper cutouts, rice, pasta

coarse salt

bubble wrap

scissors

heavy-duty aluminum foil: 9" x 11" (23 x 28 cm)

spray bottle of water

iron

fusible web: Wonder-Under

heavy interfacing: five 9" x 11" (23 x 28 cm) pieces, Peltex or Timtex

rotary cutter, acrylic ruler, and mat

backing and "hinge" fabric: 1¼ yd. (1.15 m)

sewing machine

thread

painted tabletop screen

Preparation
Cover your work surface with plastic.

Resist-Painted Stripes
Choose a colored piece of fabric for this technique. You may want to do two pieces and choose the one you like best for the finished project. Cut pieces of masking tape the length of the fabric and tear the pieces into two long strips with irregular widths. Press the tape onto the fabric. Using Lumiere paint, brush paint between the tape strips until the exposed fabric is covered. Remove the tape and let the fabric dry.

Painted Plaid
On dampened white fabric, paint two colors of Dye-na-Flow in parallel lines. While the first colors are still wet, paint a third color across the first lines to blend the colors, leaving some white space for the paint to bleed into. Let dry.

Sun Print

Cover a dampened, colored fabric piece (7" [18 cm] square) with dark colored Dye-na-Flow paint. Place a leaf, paper cutout, rice or pasta, coarse lace, or other mask on top of the painted fabric and press down so the edges are tight to the surface. Put out in direct sun and let dry. When the fabric is dry, the mask shapes should be the color of the original fabric and the background should be dark. Trim the square to 5" or 6" (12.5 or 15 cm).

Salt Patterning

Paint the entire surface of dampened white fabric with Dye-na-Flow. It should be quite wet. Throw coarse salt onto the wet paint and allow it to dry without disturbing it. The salt will pull the paint into interesting patterns.

Continued

Bubble Wrap Print

With the sponge brush and one or two colors of Lumiere paint, brush paint onto the raised side of bubble wrap. Place colored fabric facedown over the bubble wrap and press the back with your hand. Remove the fabric and let dry.

Paint Over Pleated Foil

Cut a piece of heavy-duty aluminum foil the same size as a piece of white fabric. Spray the fabric to dampen it. Fold the foil and fabric together into 1" (2.5 cm) accordion pleats. Pull out the pleats so you have peaks and valleys, and set it on the plastic-covered table. Paint one color of Dye-na-Flow paint on the peaks and another color in the valleys until the colors start to blend. Spray with more water if you want to encourage more blending. Allow to dry on the foil.

1

Heat set all of the fabric pieces by ironing them from the back for 30 seconds on all areas. Fuse the painted pieces to the interfacing with Wonder-Under, following the manufacturer's directions. With a rotary cutter, ruler, and mat, measure and cut five pieces of backing fabric the same size and fuse to the back of the interfacing pieces. Trim the "pages" down to 8" x 10" (20.5 x 25.5 cm). Fuse the sun print to one of the painted pieces. Stitch around the edges of the sun print and all of the pages using a close zigzag stitch.

2

Cut a 19" x 42" (48.5 x 106.5 cm) piece of hinge fabric. Fold the hinge right sides together lengthwise and sew around the raw edges with a ¼" (6 mm) seam, leaving a 3" (7.5 cm) opening. Trim the corners and turn right side out through the opening; press. Lay the "pages" on the hinge so the ends match and there is a tiny space between the pages. Sew down each side of the pages through all the layers.

Susan Suggests

When you design small pieces such as the ones in this project, make extras and put them in a plastic bin marked "Miscellaneous." Then when you start a new project or collage, you will have assorted items already prepared. Even things you don't like can be used as backgrounds for stamping, needle felting, or layering.

Susan Stein 2008

no-sew matted assemblage

Misty Fuse is a fusible web that is very sheer and not sticky, so you can layer up netting, lace, or other open weave fabrics with ease.

The fusible web will not come up through the holes or stiffen the fabric. Collect mementos of an event or highlight a favorite fabric motif, even trap dried materials under netting for an unusual look.

materials and tools

8½" by 11" (21.5 x 28 cm) piece of sheer fabric such as tulle, bridal netting, or a chiffon scarf

inkjet photo transfer fabric sheets or 8½" by 11" (21.5 x 28 cm) piece of fabric for background

photo on the computer or an 8" by 10" (20 x 25.5 cm) print (optional)

inkjet copier or computer printer (optional)

cheesecloth colored with dye or paint

ribbons or trims

buttons, ticket stubs, or other mementos (optional)

silk or dried flowers, leaves, or grass (optional)

cut-outs from printed fabric (optional)

two 8½" by 11" (21.5 x 28 cm) pieces of Misty Fuse fusible web

cooking parchment

clear drying fabric glue

11" by 14" (28 x 35.5 cm) precut mat with an opening approximately 8" by 10" (20 x 25.5 cm)

8½" by 11" (21.5 x 28 cm) piece of batting

cardboard cut slightly larger than the assemblage

no-sew matted assemblage

Print an 8" by 10" (20 x 25.5 cm) photo onto fabric on the computer or copier and lay aside to dry. Or you can cut a 8½" x 11" (21.5 x 28 cm) piece of fabric for your background. Cut a piece of Misty Fuse the same size. Iron the Misty Fuse on top of the background or photo, using parchment paper over the top to protect the iron.

Note: It's always a good idea to put a piece of cooking parchment under the background in case some fusible web goes beyond the edges.

Lay the mat over the background to determine how much area you have to cover. Most mats have openings less than a full 8" by 10" (20 x 25.5 cm). Arrange ribbons or trims over the Misty Fuse. Try to keep them as flat as possible. Lay on pieces of colored cheesecloth.

3

Arrange cut-out fabric motifs, dried materials, ticket stubs, commemorative buttons, award ribbons, silk flowers, etc., on top of the layers.

4

Lay a second piece of Misty Fuse over the assemblage and then cover the layers with tulle, netting, or chiffon. Cover with cooking parchment and iron to secure all the elements.

Continued

5

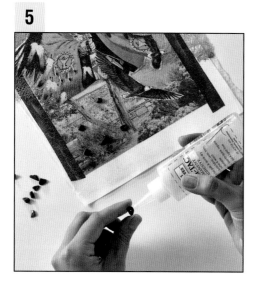

Add trims or other elements to the top of the sheer layer with fabric glue if you wish. Make sure you check the opening in your mat before gluing anything down.

6

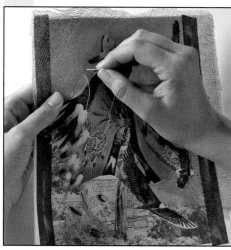

Back the assemblage with batting so it will round out the edges when you add the mat. If you want to, you can add hand stitching to accent certain elements or give texture, sewing through the assemblage and the batting.

7

Run a bead of glue around the back side of the mat opening. Place the mat carefully over the top of the assemblage and press down firmly. Place books over the top to weigh down the mat while the glue is drying.

8

Glue the cardboard on the back of the mat to cover and support the assemblage. Weigh the mat down with books until the glue dries. You can decorate the mat to coordinate with the assemblage, and be sure to sign your artwork.

Susan Suggests

Place the matted assemblage in a frame, possibly with a second mat added to set the artwork away from the glass or set a grouping of matted pieces without frames on a long, narrow shelf along with coordinating accessories.

photo-transfer mail sorter

Make a fun mail sorter for the front hall or kitchen, so each member of the family has a personal pocket.

Photo-transfer sheets—paper-backed fabric coated to make inkjet printing permanent—go right into the computer printer or copy machine. Use any printed or digital photo you have to make the centerpiece for each crazy-pieced block. Then assemble them into a wall hanging. Make one for your own family and everyone on your gift list.

materials and tools

Note: The sample is made for a six-person family; adjust the size for your own situation.

rotary cutter, acrylic ruler, and mat

fabric for front, pocket linings, and back: 1⅞ yd. (1.75 m)

six to eight pieces of coordinating prints for piecing: ¼ yd. (0.25 m)

binding fabric: ⅓ yd. (0.32 m)

double-stick tape

photos

copy paper

inkjet-photo fabric sheets: Inkjet Printing by Jacquard

copier

computer and inkjet printer (optional)

sewing machine

thread

iron

scissors

batting: 9½" x 63½" (24 x 161 cm), fusible cotton/polyester

pins

hanging stick

semitransparent inkjet fabric sheets: ExtravOrganza by Jacquard (optional)

fusible web: Mistyfuse (for ExtravOrganza)

photo-transfer mail sorter

1

With a rotary cutter, ruler, and mat, measure and cut a foundation for the pocket section from the main fabric 9½" x 63½" (24 x 161 cm).

Note: Cut the main fabric on the lengthwise grain. Cut two border pieces 2½" x 63½" (6.4 x 161 cm). For the back, cut one piece of the main fabric 13½" x 63½" (34.3 x 161 cm). Cut one 9½" (24 cm) square of lining fabric for each member of the family. Cut the piecing fabrics into 2" (5 cm)-wide strips as you need them. Cut the binding fabric into four 2" (5 cm)-wide strips.

2

Double-stick tape your photos to sheets of copy paper with space between the pictures. Place the sheets on the copier. Place the photo-transfer fabric, one sheet at a time, in the paper feed of the copier so the photos will print onto the fabric side. Print a sheet of fabric for each page of photos. Let dry. Follow the package directions if washing is needed.

3

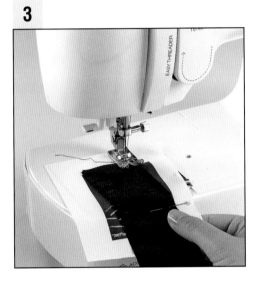

Remove the paper backing from the fabric sheets and cut them apart so you have white space around each photo. Sew one strip of fabric to the side of one photo, right sides together, using a ¼" (6 mm) seam and angling the strip. Press the strip away from the photo. Trim off the excess strip with scissors.

4

Continue to add strips at an angle to the photo, pressing the strips away from the photo, and trimming off the end of each strip as you go around the photo. Add strips until the block is more than 9½" (24 cm) square. Trim it to an exact 9½" (24 cm). Repeat for all the photos.

Continued

5

Place a lining square, right sides together, with each pieced square and sew across the top and bottom edges with a ¼" (6 mm) seam allowance. Turn right side out and press the seams to one side, and then turn the lining to the back and press flat.

6

Steam-fuse the backing to one side of the batting and steam-fuse the center panel of main fabric to the middle of the batting on the other side.

7

Lay the top pocket on the fabric 2¼" (5.5 cm) from the top edge of the center panel. Pin through all the layers. Continue to pin the pockets to the hanging 1" (2.5 cm) apart until you reach the bottom. There should be 2¼" (5.5 cm) left at the bottom. Topstitch across the bottoms of the pockets through all the layers.

8

Pin the border strips right sides together over the raw edges of the center piece and pockets. Sew through all the layers with a ¼" (6 mm) seam. Press the borders away from the pockets onto the batting. Bind the edges, add a casing on the back, insert the hanging stick, and hang.

Susan Suggests

If you want to add names to each pocket, use semitransparent ExtravOrganza photo transfer fabric to make labels on your computer. Back the organza with Mistyfuse fusible web, and iron onto the pockets.

quilted/painted folder briefcase

Set yourself apart as a creative, interesting, yet professional, person at your next committee meeting.

Sized to hold several file folders, this tote will have them wondering how you made such a unique fabric. Simple quilting, and then painting afterward, creates a wonderful texture and pattern.

Try small samples of different combinations. If you like them all, make a tote for every organization you belong to!

materials and tools

plastic cover for the table

rotary cutter, acrylic ruler, and mat

outer fabric: ½ yd. (0.5 m)

backing fabric: ½ yd. (0.5 m)

lining fabric: ½ yd. (0.5 m)

batting: 15" x 22" (38 x 56 cm), fusible by Hobbs

iron

sewing machine and walking foot or darning foot

thread

bath towel

clothes dryer

paint: Textile Color, Neopaque, or Lumiere by Jacquard

soft rubber brayer (available at craft and art supply stores)

pocket fabric: 5½" (14 cm) square (see step 4 for suggestions)

pins

ribbons: 1⅝ yd. (1.5 m) each of two different grosgrain ribbons for handles (one narrow, one wide)

embellishments for handle: yarn or trim, charms, beads (optional)

quilted/painted folder briefcase

Preparation
Cover your work surface with plastic.

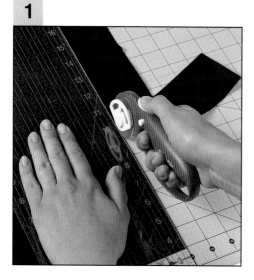

1

With a rotary cutter, ruler, and mat, measure and cut a piece of the outer fabric and a piece of backing 15" x 22" (38 x 56 cm). Cut a lining piece 14" x 21" (35.5 x 53.5 cm).

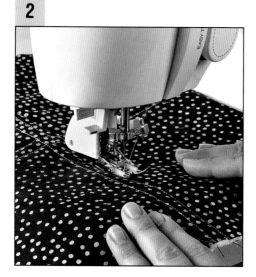

2

Fuse the quilt sandwich together by using an iron to steam the backing to the batting and then steaming the outer fabric to the other side of the batting. Quilt all over the sandwich with a simple grid or other design, using a walking foot for machine-guided straight lines or a darning foot for free-motion curved lines. The pattern should be dense and consistent. Rinse the quilt sandwich in warm water to shrink the batting a little, blot in a towel, and dry in the dryer.

3

With the brayer, apply paint lightly over the surface of the quilt sandwich, covering the raised areas. You may want to practice with the brayer first to determine how much paint you want on it when you start printing. Allow the paint to dry. Heat set the paint with a dry iron. Trim the quilt sandwich to 14" x 21" (35.5 x 53.5 cm). Press the sandwich in half, wrong sides together, to create a guideline for handle and pocket placement.

4

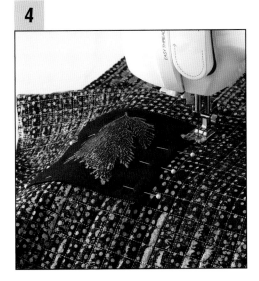

The pocket can be a piece of artwork, a photo of your dog, another piece of quilting, or just a great chunk of fabric. To line the pocket, place it right sides together with a square of lining fabric and sew across the top and bottom edges with a ¼" (6 mm) seam. Turn the pocket right side out and press. Place it in the center of one side of the quilt sandwich and pin. Sew along the bottom edge.

Rubber stamp by Fred B. Mullett

Continued

5

Sew the narrow ribbon to the center of the wide ribbon. Starting at the fold, pin the sewn ribbon to the tote: cover ¼" (6 mm) of the sides of the pocket, extend to the top of the tote, allow 7" (18 cm) for a handle, start down the other side of the pocket, repeat the placement on the other side of the fold, and finish at the fold again. Turn under the raw edge of the ribbons and pin over the starting end. Sew down both sides of the ribbon, starting and ending 1" (2.5 cm) from the top edges. Embellish the handle with yarn, trim, charms, or beads, if desired.

6

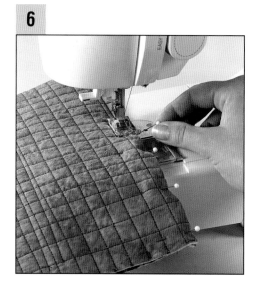

Sew the sides of the tote, right sides together, with a ¼" (6 mm) seam. Turn right side out.

7

Sew the lining in the same way, but leave a 3" or 4" (7.5 or 10 cm) opening in one side. Slip the outer tote into the lining, right sides together, and pin the raw edges, keeping the handles out of the way. Sew all around the top edge.

8

Pull the tote right side out through the opening in the lining seam. Sew the opening closed and press the tote and lining. Push the lining into the tote and topstitch around the upper edge, catching the handles for reinforcement. Buy some colored file folders to match your new tote!

Susan Suggests

Make your tote from a dark-colored quilt sandwich, and color it with this interesting technique. Working in a well-ventilated area, mix equal parts textile paint and discharge paste (both by Jacquard). Apply the mixture to the fabric (by brushing, rolling, or stamping), and allow it to dry. The discharge paste will remove the black color from the fabric and add the new color at the same time. Iron the quilt to reveal the new color.

more techniques

Try these techniques to color or embellish your fabric. Then use the fabric to make some of the projects in this book.

Freeform Monoprinting

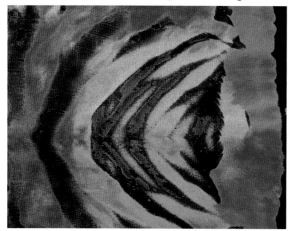

1. Cut two edges off a clear plastic sheet protector, leaving one connected edge. Open the sheet protector on a plastic-covered table. Shake or stir metallic fabric paint thoroughly, and spoon the paint onto one side of the plastic. Use two or three colors that coordinate with or complement each other.

2. Close the sheet protector. Manipulate the paint by pushing with your fingers so paint covers most of the area inside the plastic. Work quickly so the paint does not bead up or start to dry. Open the sheet protector.

3. Place one piece of fabric on each side of the sheet protector, then close it. Quickly and gently rub both sides of the plastic to transfer the paint to the fabric. Do not push the paint into the grain of the fabric or the colors will appear dull.

4. Remove the fabric pieces from the sheet protector and separate them. Let them dry flat on the plastic-covered table for 24 hours. Heat set the paint with a dry iron.

Paint Resists

Glue Resist

Create a pattern on fabric with washable glue. Let the glue dry completely. Paint the fabric with medium-bodied textile paint, using a sponge brush. Spray the painted fabric lightly with water if you would like the colors to blend. Let dry for 24 hours. Heat set the paint with a dry iron. Soak the fabric to soften the glue, and then hand wash using a toothbrush to help remove the glue. Where the glue drawings covered the fabric, the original color will appear.

Rubber-Band Resist

Pick up a piece of dampened fabric from the center. Secure rubber bands around two or more sections about 1½" (3.8 cm) apart. Dab paint into the folds with a sponge brush, using plenty of paint. Transparent paint will bleed between sections and medium-bodied paint will be more contained by the rubber-band resist. Let the fabric sit for 15 minutes or longer. Cut the rubber bands and unfold the fabric. When dry, heat set the paint with a dry iron.

Stamping with Objects

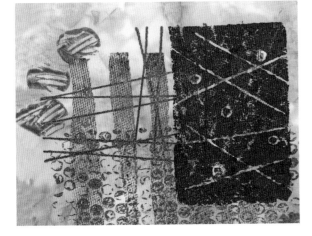

Button Stamping

Glue a button to the lid of an old pill bottle or film canister. Dip the button into a thin layer of paint, then stamp the fabric. For a distinct image, load the stamp with paint each time you use it. For varied brightness, stamp two or three times before reloading.

Incised Styrofoam Stamping

Cut a rectangle from a Styrofoam tray. With a ballpoint pen or toothpick, draw lines in the foam. Dab paint onto the foam surface with a sponge brush. Turn the foam carved side down on the fabric, and rub the back to transfer the paint to the fabric. Test first—the foam will hold more paint the second time you use it.

String Stamping

Wrap a Plexiglas or cardboard scrap with string. Hold the stamp by one of the strings on the back and dip the front into a thin layer of paint. Stamp the fabric.

Carved-Eraser Stamping

Carve a white eraser into your own one-of-a-kind design. Dip the stamp into a thin layer of paint, then stamp the fabric.

Shaving Cream Marbling

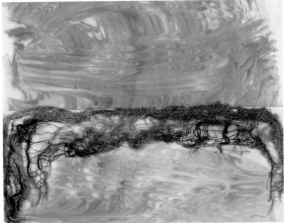

1. Spread enough shaving cream on a plastic surface, 1" (2.5 cm) deep, to match the size of your fabric. Smooth the top with a ruler—the top does not need to be level, just smooth.

2. Dribble straight lines of transparent paint onto the surface of the foam with a pipette or eyedropper. Use as many colors as you like.

3. Starting at one side, draw a coarse comb or hair pick across the lines of paint, moving from the top edge to the bottom. Wipe any shaving cream off the comb. Then comb from the bottom to top. Keep reversing direction as you create your design.

4. Drape a piece of fabric facedown onto the surface of the foam. Press it very gently into the foam so the paint adheres to the fabric. Carefully lift the fabric off the foam and scrape the excess foam from the fabric using the ruler. Comb through the paint left on the foam and make more prints until the foam is used up, adding more paint as needed. Let the paint dry and then heat set with a dry iron. Rinse and dry the fabric pieces to remove the shaving cream.

Influences
by Doroth Mayer

Photo transfer, rust-dyeing.

Fantasy Vine
by Susan Stein

More than twenty different
techniques on leaves.

Hot & Spicy
by Susan Stein

Collage, ribbon netting.

StarBuilder Mariner's Compass
by Laura Murray

Paintstiked and fused using Laura's new rubbing tools.

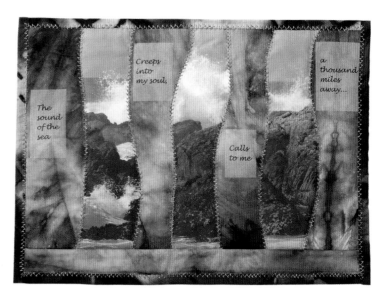

Asilomar Reverie
by Susan Stein

Photo transfer.

Dye-na-Flow Sampler
by Susan Stein

Nine different Dye-na-Flow painting techniques.

Feather Discharge
by Sue Kelly

Discharge and paint.

Leaf Montage
by Susan Stein

Rubber stamping, screen printing, and sun printing
by Diane Bartels; shibori dyeing by Deb Lunn;
overdyed background by Wendy Richardson.

ing
by Tina Hughes

Various techniques.

Silk Surprises
by Susan Stein

Lasagna dyeing with Dye-na-Flow.

2008 Journal Class Samples
by Tina Hughes

Various techniques.

Orchid
by Elizabeth Palmer-Spilker

Photo transfer.

about the author

Susan Stein started quilting in 1977 and has delighted in getting other people obsessed with quilting and surface design ever since. This former president and show chairman for Minnesota Quilters was named Minnesota Quilter of the Year in 2003. An energetic and passionate quilter, Susan has shared her talents as the author of four books and as a contributing author to numerous others. She has taught many classes in Minnesota and around the country. Many of the hundreds of quilts produced by her hands serve as wall hangings, publication pieces, and store samples, while others are on public display or in personal use. Susan co-owned a quilt shop from 1980 to 1985 and opened her current shop, Colorful Quilts and Textiles, in 1995.

Resources

Angelina and Angelina Film
www.embellishmentvillage.com
877-639-9820

Foil, foil adhesive, paintstiks, StarBuilder rubbing templates
www.lauramurraydesigns.com

Gel Medium
Golden Artist Colors Gel Mediums Regular Gel (matte)
Available at art supply stores

Jacquard paints, discharge paste, Pearl Ex powders, inkjet printing fabric sheets, ExtravOrganza fabric sheets, textile medium
www.jacquardproducts.com
800-442-0455

Paintstiks, rubbing plates, Grip-n-Grip sheets
www.quiltingarts.com
Printed images
Carol Belanger Grafton, ed., *Authentic Chinese Cut-Paper Designs*, Dover Design Library
(New York: Dover Publications, Inc., 1988)

Silk fabric and scarves
www.thaisilks.com
800-722-7455

Silk fiber
www.treenwaysilks.com
888-383-7455

Wool beads, charms
www.artgirlz.com
866-507-4822

index